ACKNOWLEDGMENTS

I would like to thank the following people for their unwavering support, devotion and commitment. For being part of an extraordinary and memorable part of my journey. For your team effort, whether in collaboration in the making of this book or ultimately helping to magically bring old St. Nick to life. Simply put, I couldn't have done it without you.

Evalani B.
Paulette K.
Mamo O.
Hugh G.
Mariam M.
Renee G.
Cara C.

With enormous appreciation and gratitude. A warm mahalo.

DEDICATION

To My Mother

MARY E. RUSSELL BOYCE

With Love

CHRISTMAS STORIES WITH SANTA

My Life as Jolly Old St. Nick

BY

DONALD A. BOYCE

12 - 25 - 2019

TO THE VENABLE OHANA
(Family) & We Hope you Have

MELE KALIKIMAKA

A Wonderful 2020 & A Lot More to
Come

ALOHA e ENJOY

EVERYONE AT THE NORTH POLE
WOODWORKERS, COOKS, BAKERS & ALL THE
WONDERFUL ELVES want to Wish X
& THANK YOU FOR ALL THE GOOD YOU
ALL YEAR LONG
WE LOVE YOU & ALL YOUR

MAHALO NUI LOA

FRIENDS @ QVC & MAY GOD BLS
SANTA DONALD
YOU & YOURS AND ENJOY ALL THE
LOVE THAT WE GIV
XMAS, SANTA

Contents

IN HAWAIIAN

MELE KALIKIMAKA
Merry Christmas

HAUOLI MAKAHIKI HOU
Happy New Year

MAHALO
THANK you

MAHALO Nui Loa
THANK You Very much

OHANA
Family

ALOHA
Hello, Goodby, I Love you

Aloha DAVID

Santa David

THE STORY OF SANTA a.k.a. DONALD AVARD BOYCE

On the eventful morning of June 7, 1939, a baby was born to Mary E. Russell Boyce and Charles Avard Boyce in the town of Murry, Utah. A baby, hopefully, destined for good things. That baby was me - Donald Avard Boyce, eventually to be known and loved as "Santa". This is the story of how I came to be Santa and some of the amazing, touching, funny, unforgettable memories I made along the way.

A SANTA IN THE MAKING

I had a pretty normal childhood, did regular kid activities, and attended school like everyone else. Like many neighboring farms and folks nearby, we lived on a 16 acre ranch just south of Salt Lake City, at the mouth of Big Mountain Wood Canyon, which at the time was called Butlerville. On our ranch we had the usual livestock, including cows, horses, chickens, turkeys, goats, pigs, rabbits, in addition to the common domestic dog. However, what set our family apart from the rest was the unique animal I had as a pet. To my knowledge, I was the only one in the entire Salt Lake Valley that had a Golden Eagle bird as a pet! I remember riding my quarter horse, placing the eagle on my left shoulder, then racing up the street - causing the winds to lift her wings - where she could fly the short distance of about twenty feet before coming in for landing. Goldie – the name I gave her – had a broken wing that she never fully recovered from. It was a cold winter day when my grandfather and I found the tiny bird flapping on the ground. We'd decided to go hunting for rabbits when something caught my eye.

• • •

"A bird." I knelt down to get a better look.

"You know what kind of bird that is, don't you Donald?" Grandfather asked. "It's an eaglet. Had it not been for the snow, that eaglet would probably have died. It softened the fall for the little guy."

I brought the tiny bird home and fed it every day while doing my best to nurse it back to health. Eventually she became a full grown adult eagle weighing in at about 13 pounds with a six and a half foot wingspan. Unfortunately, she never fully recovered from her broken wing and was never able to fly more than about 20 feet at the most. Nonetheless, Goldie was strong and beautiful and had grown such a strong connection and bond with me. We had built up a wonderful level of trust. In return, I was very fond of her too - we were a pair! It was during this prominent time in my life, when I turned 17 years old in June of 1956, that mother came to me and asked if I could play Santa for the annual party that my family held every year during the Christmas holidays.

"Why isn't one of the uncles going to play Santa again?" I asked, puzzled as to why the family tradition couldn't continue the same way it always did. I signaled for Goldie with a quick lift of my arm, a delicacy of worms in my hand, before the majestic creature swooped in for a landing and perched upon my arm to feast.

"I think it's time we give everyone something new to remember. The kids are beginning to recognize that it's one of the uncles under the Santa suit." She shook her head then looked at me, "It's time we change things up. Time to give them a surprise." Her face beamed with the idea, "The last thing they'll expect is you."

"But I don't want to, Mother," I protested. "I don't feel like playing Santa." I shook my head no, mesmerized by the magnificent bird who had now fully stretched out her golden wings.

"Donald," she said, in the typical mother-knows-best-sort-of-way, "I think you should."

We all know how mothers can be; mine was no different, and at some point shortly thereafter, I unwittingly obliged.

Evidently, my parents had already gone ahead and quickly picked out a Santa suit for me and let me tell you, it was the most horrible suit I'd ever seen! It was made of felt and itchy imitation wool. I had ugly, plastic leggings that were pulled up over my shoes with little patches of fluff. If that wasn't bad enough, I had a scroungy-looking beard that attached over my ears with two plastic hooks - much like reading glasses do – and hung down over my mouth and nose area. A sad-looking suit, no doubt!

I went to the party. I entered through the back door where there were gifts and presents in a red pillowcase set off to the side. I popped in and gave the traditional "Ho, Ho, Ho and Merry Christmas" to all of the guests. I then took a seat at one of the chairs and began to call names for each person to come up. Everyone took turns sitting on Santa's lap and received a Christmas gift with their name on it. I can still remember so clearly towards the end of Santa's visit a young neighborhood boy who's turn was next.

"Come on up here," I said in my best jolly Santa voice as I leaned over and lifted him onto my lap. "What's your name?" I asked the little boy who couldn't be more than three or four years old. He told me his name - although I can't remember it after all these years – but what stood out most and what I do remember is how bad this little boy was shaking in his boots. His body trembled as his wide eyes sat transfixed upon me.

"Are you afraid of Santa?" I asked the trembling boy, fully expecting to hear a resounding yes or the very least, a violent nod! But, what I got in return was priceless.

"Oh no!" The little neighborhood boy's eyes began to tear up now and he shook his head. "No, Santa!" he was adamant. " I love you!" he emphasized and repeated over and over again. "I love you, Santa!" he said, placing his little arms around me for a hug.

I sat feeling elated with a warmth that filled my soul. For me, it was a defining moment. When I saw my own reflection in the eyes of a child who's heart was overflowing with love for Santa, I knew there was something magical happening, something far more profound than merely playing a jolly character in a red suit. And so it began. My journey and the making of Santa Claus.

Three years after playing Santa for the family Christmas Party, I was called on a mission by the Church of Jesus Christ and Latter Day Saints, more commonly known as the Mormons. This mission took me to beautiful Hawaii, where for the next two years I would be kept busy talking to and converting people who were interested in Mormonism. Although I've played Santa for over 55 years, there are a few sporadic years in between where Santa took a backseat. These were two of those years.

After my mission, I remained in Hawaii and got married, settling into family life while keeping the spirit of Santa alive through my own kids. Soon, I was back in the suit playing Santa for various events during the holidays.

When I first began playing Santa in these early years, I wore a fake beard. It wasn't an inexpensive beard either! But, for both myself and my wife, we had made the commitment that I would be the best Santa out there - no matter what! That meant investing in Santa. At one time I worked with the set director of the Rockettes in New York and bought a set of wigs from him all made of yak hair. Each set cost more than $400, but all in all, it was worth it. At the end of each holiday season, my wife would take the wigs to the hair salon to be washed, curled and all ready for the following year. Perfect!

One year, I had the brilliant idea to grow my own beard. Hair grows about an inch a month, so before too long I had a pretty good size beard just in time for holidays. The only problem was, my beard wasn't white. However, my wife didn't see a problem with that at all - as far as she was concerned, there was nothing that a visit to the hair salon couldn't cure! So off we went to the local hair salon where we decided to have my beard whitened.

I can still feel the burning on my scalp from the hair dying process; the smell of the chemicals infiltrating my nostrils due to my thick mustache right above my lip. I endured this process with each passing year, until finally I said I'd had enough. For over 11 years, I grew and used my own hair, my own beard, my own eyebrows, applying a little rouge on my cheeks and nose, but not much of anything else. I wear half glasses to add to the overall Santa image, which completes the look perfectly.

HERE COMES SANTA ON A CHRISTMAS CANOE!

Playing the role of Old St. Nick for 16 years at a particular hotel in Waikiki, I'd have to say, I absolutely loved every minute of it. At its sister hotel, also in Waikiki, I played Santa for 20 years, 18 of which I rode into shore in style at Waikiki Beach on the famous Santa Christmas Canoe, flanked by the beach boys paddling me past the surfers all the way to the beach. Like every year before it, a wonderful celebration had begun way before our canoe even touched the shoreline! The music could be heard clear out in the ocean and rang out through the air as a local band played a string of familiar Christmas melodies with wonderful crowd participation joining in to sing along. The keiki ("children" in Hawaiian) adorn and draped in beautiful flower leis happily sang and shared some of the traditional hula dances with the cheering crowd. It was always a festive and memorable celebration with so much fun had by all as they waited in anticipation for the excited moment and the arrival of Santa.

"If I could draw your attention towards the ocean at this time…" the MC would say over loud speakers to the cheering folks who quickly ran - some even toppling over onto the sand – and squeezed into any empty space in the growing crowd; cameras and iPhones ready to snap away! "I think if we all join in and sing jingle bells together and we sing loud enough, we just might see Santa's canoe coming!"

"Jingle bells, jingle bells, jingle all the way…" the festive crowd sang loud, "Oh what fun it is to ride…." And the singing then turned to voices of cheering, whistling, screaming and applause as Santa's canoe came into view. "Santa!" It's Santa! I see him! I see him!" the children were ecstatic, pointing at the ocean. "Santa! Santa!" they screamed with joy, jumping up and down as they immediately flash mobbed and surrounded the canoe after Santa's Christmas Crew caught a perfect wave that brought the canoe right onto shore!

"Mele Kalikimaka! ("Merry Christmas" in Hawaiian) Mele Kalikimaka! Ho, Ho, Ho! Merry Christmas! Merry Christmas!" Santa gave a huge shaka sign as the Christmas Canoe Crew - decked out in the traditional red and white Christmas hat and attire - made landfall, then escorted Santa up onto the beach. Flashes came from cameras at every angle as Santa waved hello to the bustling crowd before taking his seat in the center of the stage area. The happy crowd enjoyed more entertainment of dancing and music and tried to get as many photos of the

Hawaiian Santa as they could. After a time of meet and greets, the crowd would then follow Santa into the hotel where a line had already formed by folks wanting to be first to sit, chit chat and have their picture taken with Santa. Children and adults alike made their way into the main lobby and wasted no time making their request for Christmas that year: a boyfriend for mommy, a real pony, two ducks, some fish, birds, puppies, kimonos, a boat for my son. A bigger boat for his dad! The entire morning was a celebration of laughter and Christmas cheer that happily became a tradition that lasted almost two decades!

One year after I arrived on shore, a local lady wearing a pretty Hawaiian floral dress recalled how she came to hear about the Santa in the canoe. "I remember seeing Santa on T.V.," she said after catching it on the local news channel the year before. "I was busy making dinner for my family and my keiki started yelling, Santa! Santa!" she reminisced. "I turned off the stove to sit and watch it with them and they asked why they didn't get to see Santa come in on the canoe too? So, I called around and found all the info I needed so that the following year – this year - my kids would be right here in Waikiki, on the shore, screaming for Santa coming in on the canoe," she laughed. "Look at them!" she nodded proudly at the little boy and girl splashing around in the seashore hoping to be one of the first to spot Santa's canoe. "I made it happen."

The Hawaii Visitors and Convention Bureau had relayed numerous accounts of excited fans across the country calling in to their offices over the years. They were inquiring about the Hawaiian Santa that came into Waikiki beach on none other than a wooden canoe!

" I found myself really missing Hawaii when I caught the late night news and saw that Hawaiian Santa Claus coming into Waikiki beach on his canoe!" a woman from North Carolina said. "Gosh, that looked like so much fun. And the crowd went berserk!"

Such music to my ears. Apparently that news footage taken during Christmas every year as Santa came into Waikiki on his wooden canoe would find its way clear across the country and seen around the world for the next 18 years as Santa and his Christmas canoe crew went viral!

Another couple from Nebraska had rounded up the entire family to include grandma and grandpa too! They strategically planned a Hawaii Christmas Vacation around the arrival of the Santa coming in on the canoe.

"We just had to come! I'm glad we finally made it!" the grandfather of the family chuckled, "We weren't going to miss this for the world! Even if it took us a couple years to get here!" he said, finding it difficult to sit still in his lounge chair fully aware of the beach crowd of excited Santa fans growing bigger by the second. A roped off section made of flower leis bordered and secured the path reserved in anticipation for jolly old St. Nick to make his way easily up onto the beach and into the happy crowd.

It's funny, I recall a cute story that the social director of one of these hotels told me one year. He and his family had decided to do some last minute Christmas shopping at the shopping center.

"Look sweetheart, there's Santa," he said to his five-year-old daughter as they passed a column of life-size candy canes. "Why don't you go on over and have your picture taken."

The little girl turned to her father disconcertingly as if what he had said was an abomination. "No," she shook her head vehemently. "That's *not* the real Santa! The real Santa comes to your hotel. And he comes on a canoe!" Needless to say, she did not take a picture with him and was actually one of the first people front and center amongst a huge crowd that had gathered on the shores of Waikiki Beach awaiting Santa's arrival a few days later. The real Santa!

HAWAIIAN SHAKA SANTA

A call came into my office in June of 2017. I had the honor of being invited to do a photo shoot as Santa with the prestigious Hokule'a. For those who are not aware, the Hokule'a is the infamous Polynesian double-hulled voyaging canoe. Overseen and launched by the Polynesian Voyaging Society, this canoe has traveled to many places throughout the world, including a three year world tour – ending in a Mahalo ("thank you" in Hawaiian) tour that brought it back through Hawaiian waters, ultimately resting at the majestic Waikiki Beach.

I got a lot of attention while at a popular hotel on Waikiki Beach where I had changed into my Santa suit to get ready for the photo shoot, I walked across the driveway and parking structure to cut through yet another driveway to reach another hotel, from where I made my way down the main lobby of surprised guests. The tourists and visitors couldn't resist stopping to see what all the commotion was about. It wasn't every day that festive sounds of jingle bells could be heard ringing loudly through the main lobby. Especially not in the summer!

● ● ●

"Whoa! Santa!" They cheered, followed by a quick look of perplexity. "What in the world are you doing here?" They laughed snapping away with their cameras and iPhones. "You're a bit early aren't you Santa?" they finally asked.

"Well," I started, "I have my list, I brought it with me right here," patting my pocket for dramatic effect, "and I'm just checking to see that you're all on the nice list and not the naughty list." I gave a jolly laugh. "And I am keeping score!" I gave a wave and continued onto my photo shoot appointment. We went out on a canoe and took a bunch of photos over the course of the next two hours. The image pictured here is one of my favorites, as this was one of many fun memories as Santa.

KOA WOOD AND CRAFT FAIRS

I have always enjoyed creativity in all its forms, and for years I worked as a wood artist, using the rare and beautiful Koa wood, specializing in custom picture frames, jewelry boxes, clocks, vases, pens, rocking chairs and other furniture, watches, and more. Every year after visiting family for Thanksgiving dinner, we would get home just in time to hit-the-sack early as the traditional annual Christmas Craft Fair in Honolulu would be held very early the following morning. We had to be up and on the road at the crack of dawn. One year while we were attending the Christmas Craft Fair to sell my koa crafts and offer photos with Santa, a small family of three approached me.

"We have a special request," the woman asked politely.

"Okay," I said, "Please, tell me what it is."

"Mother, please let me tell the story," The man insisted.

"By all means."

"You see, " the man began thoughtfully, "I was born in June. In December when I was six months old I went to meet Santa and have my photo taken with him for the first time." He continued, "Every year after that, I had to go and get a picture taken with Santa." He paused for a moment. "Little did I know what my mother was doing at the time, but it was part of her little ritual - I had to go have my picture taken with Santa during December. It was a little embarrassing in high school when I had to leave school a little early to go to the mall and have a picture taken with Santa." He chuckled and hung his head, "It was even more embarrassing in college when I had to have a picture taken with Santa. Currently, I have at least 20 different pictures taken with 20 different Santa Claus' at various places over the years."

Everyone had a good laugh, his mother giggling, reminiscing at the story.

"I'm getting married in June of next year," the man finally added. "The wedding will take place right here in Hawaii, on the island of Kauai."

His mother quickly chimed in, "Now, let me tell you what I have done." She smiled, "I've taken every picture he's had with Santa and put it in a book. When he gets married next year in Hawaii, we're going to take the book of him with Santa from the time he was born until now, and we're going to present it to his new wife. Because we're in Hawaii, we want a picture with a Hawaiian Santa - he could either be sitting on your lap, standing next to you, or even shaking your hand?"

"Of course," I quickly agreed. "That's a great idea."

"Thank you," she happily replied, then turned to her son and sighed, "Well, I guess that'll be the end of our tradition. Guess you could say we've come full circle."

"What do you mean?" He turned to her, "Do you think this is the end? It's only the beginning! You started something fantastic. A wonderful tradition that I have every intention of carrying on with my own children."

As I listened, I thought *how great a tradition* is that? It struck me how prominent and memorable a role Santa plays in so many lives and households throughout the world.

NOT YOUR AVERAGE SHOPPING MALL SANTA

As I look back over the years of playing the role of Santa, it was always important for me to uphold myself with integrity and to always conduct myself in such a way when interacting and engaging with the children who came to see me every Christmas holiday. I wasn't your typical "shopping mall" Santa who muttered very few words to the family or hardly engaged with the kids or a mall Santa who ran on autopilot or worked an assembly line that basically went as follows: sit with children, smile for camera, next kid in line, repeat. It's such a sad fact, but there is nothing worse than a person who is representing Old Saint Nick who has no desire to even be there at all, except to earn some money. We've all seen them before, right? A bored, sloppy, disengaged Santa who looks at his watch more than the kids who come to visit him and who probably got his costume from a package in one of those seasonal Halloween thrift shops, probably from the same mall! I'm proud to say that definitely was never me! Playing Santa meant so much more. Half the joy of playing the role of Santa were the children.

It never mattered how long the line was. I would take as much time as I needed to talk and listen to the child and give him or her a moment to share a little about themselves. They enthusiastically spoke of ballet recitals and swim lessons, karate tournaments and spelling bees. They spoke of favorite teachers and silly siblings, funny friends and goofy pets, which would eventually lead – of course – to what they wanted for Christmas that year.

I recall one little girl who's excitement went through the roof when I shared my take on using mathematics to feed my reindeers! She had a love for numbers. Her favorite subject was math, and when I told her how important math was in every area of life she sat all ears and listened intensely.

"Why, I even use math to feed the reindeers!" I said, as a matter of fact.

"You do?" she asked, her huge blue eyes glued to mine with amazement and wonder.

"Of course! I measure the reindeers' food on a scale and each reindeer gets the same amount of food every day. If I didn't measure it, I might give too much food and before you know it, the reindeers will gain too much weight!" I frowned, "Why just last week, Prancer was close to going on a diet after he had a little too much to eat," I explained.

"But Santa, didn't you say you measure it on the scale?" she asked thoughtfully.

"Why, yes I do. But, " I leaned in and whispered to her, "Prancer's been sneaking food from Dasher's dinner bowl." I gave a disapproving sigh.

She gave the sweetest, toothless grin and giggled.

"If the reindeers get too fat, then they wouldn't be able to pull Santa's heavy sleigh." I frowned, "And we wouldn't want that to happen now would we?"

"No Santa, we wouldn't," the little girl shook her head. "Because then there would be no one to deliver presents to all the boys and girls on Christmas Eve!" she concluded.

"You're right." I tapped the tip of her nose, "But don't you worry, that will *never* happen." I reassured her. "Not with math there to help us, thank goodness!" I gave a sigh of relief.

A funny incident I recall is the time when pee ran down my leg from a child who was far too busy going through his personal Christmas list and quite frankly had no time for anyone or anything to interrupt him - even if nature called! And nature was calling! Hollering! Screaming even! Texting, skyping, you name it! Heck, it even left a voicemail!

With my fair share of mishaps, there were just as many incredible experiences with children who were clearly on a mission when they showed up for their visit with Santa. To say they were beautifully dressed to the nine would be an understatement! There were dazzling fairies and Christmas princesses, nutcracker soldiers and cowboys - complete with boots, hat and lasso of course. But I have to admit that some of my favorites were the little 'Santas' that waltzed in fully decked out from head to toe in gorgeous Santa suits, with added touches of silver and gold garland that sparkled on their fancy shoes. I had to stay on my 'A' game, as the competition was continually getting fierce!

Since the very beginning of my Santa days, I've quickly gotten use to babies and toddlers being thrust into my arms by excited new moms or seasoned parents. More often than not, it was the mothers who would take the time to stop, organize and adjust the children, comb their hair, and arrange them to pose, then re-arrange them again, finally getting everyone to smile pretty for the camera. However, this wasn't always the case. To be honest, there were times when I couldn't tell who was more excited - the kids or the parents.

"Hi Santa!" A woman rushed over to me, tossed her toddler to me as if the infant were a football on a football field, then quickly took a seat on one of my legs. Meanwhile, the two older children took their cue from their mom and hit the ground running, jumping up onto my lap, squeezing into any extra space they could find. With this bunch, it was every man for himself!

"Hey!" the boy and the oldest of the four started up. "I was here first!" He winced.

"No! I was here first!" The oldest of the sisters corrected while the smallest of the bunch stood in front of everyone wailing before her mother scooped her up, a fresh stream of tears and snot running down her cheeks.

"Honey, let's wipe your tears. We don't want Santa to put you on the naughty list now do we?" She stated, which only made the child scream even louder.

With children, somethings never change. Like the fact that no matter how many years go by, no matter the age or gender, in my experience, I find that children always know what they want for Christmas. Well, *most* of the time. In fact, rarely has there been a child that didn't know what he or she wanted - even though, it can certainly start out that way initially. I was Santa at the annual Christmas event for 21 years at a wonderful company and it was always fun - never a dull moment when speaking to the children.

"What do you want for Christmas?" I'd finally get to ask the little boy or little girl.

"I don't know," they would respond, clueless.

"Did you know there's only five days left till Christmas?" I questioned. "I know exactly what you need! I think you might need a bucket of wet sand!"

"What?" a stunned little boy's expression turned to laughter "Nah!" We would shake our heads simultaneously.

"Then how about a dry coconut palm?"

"No!" We'd shake our heads again, the little girl wrinkling her nose. "I don't think so." We would laugh together. Eventually they would ease into the 'what-do-I-want-for-Christmas-challenge' until they came up with just the right toy or gift they would love to have.

During my early years when I had a fake beard and ugly suit, the boys wanted trucks, cars, boots, hats, guns, GI Joe figurines, Lincoln Logs, electric toys, trains, planes, tinker toys and more. The girls wanted Barbies, bake ovens, dolls, puzzles, dresses, coloring books, and clothes. Today, the types of gifts being asked for are an entirely different ball game. Mostly electronics and iPhones, iPads, computers and so many other technological gadgets that I've never heard of in my life. Definitely different things for different times. But, not all is lost, they're talking to *Santa*, after all.

"Well," I would always say to him or her, "I'm not promising that I'll have that specific gift for you, but I promise that I will make every effort to check through my sleigh and see if I have exactly what you're asking for." A simple explanation was all that was needed in most cases and the child left satisfied, happy, smiling and hugging their parents. I could smile knowing that for most children, all is well in the world, and nothing warms my heart more.

ADULTS ONLY!

Most of the time after I had an adult sit on my lap and their picture had been taken with Santa, I would offer the option of a 'fun' picture with Santa, if they wanted.

"What is that?" they would often ask.

"You'll see once you see the picture. But, what I want you to do is kiss me on the cheek."

"What? Oh no, you're not going to turn and kiss me on the lips are you? Cause I know this trick," one unsuspecting woman laughed suspicious.

"Oh no. Of course not, I won't do that. Just kiss me on the cheek."

So when they turned to kiss me on the cheek - and of course the photographers and camera crew were prepared – I opened my mouth and took a deep breath in, giving an expression of shock and great surprise! Snap! I can't tell you how many people just got a kick out of this!

As joyful and happy-go-lucky kids are at heart, they are still human, which means at times they can be equally cranky, moody, angry and grumpy. Once, the mood swing was easily attributed to a soiled diaper that – unfortunately – wasn't caught in time. Poop oozed from a soggy diaper onto my lap. Thankfully, I was able to change out of the Santa suit pretty quickly. Unlike another time shortly thereafter when a young couple brought their newborn baby for her first picture with Santa. Piece of cake, right? Almost. Until the baby threw all of her breakfast up onto my coat.

"Oh my God!" the young mother was mortified. "I'm so sorry, Santa!"

"I told you not to feed her yet," her husband quickly put his two cents in, trying hard to clear himself of any blame.

"I just got through nursing her," she said apologetically wiping my shoulder with the baby's burp towel.

"Don't mention it," I set her at ease. "That's why I have elves." I pointed to one of my assistants who had scurried over with a clean towel. "Santa's always prepared," I told her. Unfortunately for the remainder of the visit, I had to sit with the towel draped over my Santa suit that was now covered in breast milk. At least the towel was red and matched my suit. Phew!

With all the wonderful, sweet, uplifting memorable experiences I've recalled over the fun years of playing Santa, there were equally just as many intriguing, quirky, funny and downright non-traditional experiences, too!

I cannot forget this one particular party I attended one evening in the heart of Waikiki on Kuhio Avenue. I had no reason to believe that this private party would be anything other than your typical Christmas party gathering. An ordinary phone call came in this particular day where the person on the other end, who was clearly in charge, dutifully made arrangements for an upcoming holiday gathering, asking all the typical questions about my services, what I do, my rates, my availability and general details.

Simple, right?

Well, I should have seen the signs from the get go! For starters, when I went to actually find the address, for the life of me, I could not see where the designated address was supposed to be. I drove my van up and down Kuhio Avenue again and again! For goodness sake, I could not see this specific address number. Finally, a side street parking space miraculously opened up and I swooped in, parked my van, fed the meter and with determination, set off to find this so-called-address. *It's got to be here somewhere nearby. Here's the street number before, here's the address after.* I looked down the street at the buildings, then back up again for another frustrating moment when low and behold, to my great astonishment, there it was!

A tiny building sat unobtrusively between two other towering buildings on either side of it. No wonder I couldn't find it! To make matters worse, the door to enter blended in so well, almost camouflaged, to where it was not uncommon for anyone to pass by without a second glance. I opened the tiny door, had to step through it sideways because it was so small. I looked up and instantly faced a long, dark flight of stairs of at least 20 steps that seemed to go straight up. I finally reached the top and found myself in the middle of a long hallway. I walked a few steps and thankfully found the apartment number I was looking for. I knocked on the door.

"Come in!" a voice called from inside. "Door's open!"

Nothing could prepare me for what was next. I turned the knob, opened the door and - ugh - I was shocked! To my great surprise, every single person in the room was butt-ass naked! Not a stitch of clothing on anyone! Anyone, except me.

"Surprise!" the voices shouted. "Eh, howzit Santa! We dakine, was waiting for you," they said in the pidgin slang commonly used among some island locals. "Ho! We taut you wasn't going come!" they joked cheerfully. "Come, come!" One of the girls waved me in from the doorway, "we like take peechah wit you."

What was Santa to do? They had already paid for my services. So, I did what any sensible Santa would do. I got straight to work. With an impeccable reputation to uphold and a this-should-be-interesting-attitude, I pulled up my boot straps and with complete confidence and professionalism, I stepped into the lion's den. To say it was interesting is an understatement! As the evening wore on, we snapped photos and I found myself with women on my knees and girls wrapped in my arms. Boobs in my face and buttocks in my hands!

"Santa, I never know you was going be so handsome!" she flirted openly.

"Eh!" another couple rushed her off, "neva mine! Get off, our turn for take peechah!" they said as the room roared in laughter.

When the night finally drew to a close about an hour later – one of the most uncomfortable hours I'd had – it was time to wrap it up and head out. I thanked them and stood up to leave when one of the women said,

"Where you going, Santa?" She pressed, "You cannot leave. It's your turn to take your clothes off, too!"

I laughed a hearty laugh and shook my head, "I'm sorry, but no. The deal was I would get paid to attend the Christmas party. That's it." I replied firmly with a laugh and waved good-bye. Usually it's the kids that surprise me and basically steal the show. Clearly in this situation, the adults won this round. Hands down! I went home and explained the ordeal to my wife, who stopped me mid-sentence.

"Donald, that suit goes straight to the dry cleaners right now!" she demanded. I wasn't going to argue with her on that. She marched into the local dry cleaners and had them do an extra cleaning on the suit. In by 7am and out by 5pm, in plenty of time for my next Christmas party.

COMPANY CHRISTMAS PARTY

I had been the Santa for the employee Christmas party at another event for about eight years when this funny situation took place. One year at their annual Christmas party, there was a ramp set up, featuring a beautiful sleigh sitting at the top. The company had a photographer placed off to the side for employees who wanted to get a picture with Santa. Of course, there was lots of fun festive music, games, dancing and all the ono (means delicious in Hawaiian) food you could imagine. I went to take Santa's seat inside the sleigh when the party began. A line of employees made their way slowly, one at a time, taking pictures and telling Santa why they deserved to have that new BMW car or the trip to Vegas to try their luck at hopefully hitting a jackpot worth millions. The line was moving at a steady pace when it parted dramatically.

What in the world? I thought, wondering why folks began parting like the Red Sea. Then, they came into view. Not one, but two very large, heavy-set women who painstakingly and with great determination slowly made their way up the ramp.

"Dear Lord Jesus," I began to pray. "Please do not let them be coming to have a picture taken with Santa," I asked, "together!" Well, just my luck, God was scheduled for another party that day and this frightening possibility was unfolding right before my eyes.

"Howzit Santa!" the taller of the two women made her way to the top of the ramp first "Wow! You get da nice view from up hea!" she took in the view from the stage, "Eh, hurry up, we waiting fo you!" she teased her friend who was a few steps behind.

"Den wait fo me next time Mary!" she said to her friend who practically raced up to get to Santa first.

Turns out this duo not only wanted a picture with Santa together, but they wanted to both sit on Santa's lap - at the same time. Santa in general is a pretty big guy with a bright red suit that can hardly be over-looked or easily missed for that matter, am I right? We took the picture together and after the photos had been developed, all I could say was abracadabra! Santa had completely disappeared!

Now, it's a well-known fact throughout the world that Santa is magic and has magical powers. Yes, he embodies the very essence of amazement and wonder and has performed many 'miracles' in the lives of so many children across the world. But, to *disappear* completely? Now *that's* a new record! Even for Santa! Now you see me, now you don't.

I was invited to be Santa at a another company Christmas celebration for eight years. One year, I was ushered in and sat on a stage with a big chair that had been prepared for me. One by one, each guest came up, chose a gift off the table, had a picture taken with Santa, then left the stage so the next person could come up. After a while, I noticed that after people left the stage, they began congregating in front of the stage looking up at me!

Gee, I thought, beginning to worry, when the room erupted in laughter more than once. I immediately took a quick assessment. Belt buckle together? Check. Buttons secured? Check. Zipper up? Check. Boots? Check. I hadn't unknowingly stepped on anything that I could see? Still, the voices roared in laughter and applause rang out in short intervals as the crowd in front of me got bigger by the minute.

"Mele Kalikimaka, Santa," a pretty girl said after picking out a gift and stopping over to say hello. For the folks who don't know, that's Merry Christmas in Hawaiian.

"Mele Kalikimaka to you," I greeted. "Are you just about ready for Christmas, young lady?"

"I think so," she shrugged nonchalantly. "Just a few more gifts to wrap, but other than that I think I'm in good shape." She instantly turned to the rowdy crowd below and quietly laughed.

"I have a question," I asked her.

"Yes?"

"Out of curiosity – I see them pointing and laughing – I was wondering, is it me they're laughing at?"

She turned to the crowd, then back at me, "Them?" she pointed. "Oh, no Santa. They're not laughing at you. I don't know if you knew, but there's a slide show behind you." She motioned to the big screen stationed behind my head that I wasn't aware of. "They're showing old photos and pictures of all the years when you came for the previous Christmas parties. They're actually laughing at themselves! Their old fashioned hairstyles and the outdated clothes they wore." She was giggling almost uncontrollably now.

"Phew! Thank goodness," I laughed with great relief knowing they weren't laughing *at* me but rather with me.

What? You think Santa's made of steel? Santa has feelings too! But in all seriousness, it was a fantastic party and one of the best things about being Santa is that there was never a dull moment.

I was Santa at the Christmas party for another beautiful establishment for about eight years where my family, including my wife and youngest son, may as well have been distant cousins to the prince of Dubai because we were all treated like absolute royalty!

The first year I was there, there were about seven or eight different people assigned to work alongside me. It was very organized. One 'elf ' was stationed at the door where children came in. Another elf was at the door leading back out, there was one on the stage, and yet another brought the children up to greet and meet Santa, while another escorted the child off the stage. There were also two photographers and a personal helper. This well-known company didn't skimp on the decorations either. The large open space where Santa was seated was adorned and lavishly decorated with not one, but seven towering, gorgeous Christmas trees! A magical, winter wonderland experience for everyone!

A vast majority of the older children who came to see Santa, ranging in age from 8 to 12 years old I would guess, were so over the top excited to approach me. I immediately understood their excitement when I saw the little books they were clutching.

"Santa! Can you sign my autograph book?" One girl jumped up and down ecstatically flipping through the book to the next empty page.

"Of course," I said, "but first…" I gestured to one of the kind assistants, who were always ready to sprint into action the minute I needed anything, "Where do you suppose I left my red pen?" I wondered aloud.

"I think I know exactly where you left it, Santa!" He ran over to the side, whispered something to another lady who disappeared then reappeared a second later smiling.

"Is this what you were looking for Santa?"

"That's it," I chuckled, "that's Santa's special red felt pen," I said as I took the autograph book and began writing inside.

December 24, 2017

Mele Kalikimaka.

A big Aloha to you.

Have a nice Christmas.

Love from Santa

It was a while before the crowd of children dissipated and they broke off into little groups and clusters around the room, laughing and comparing their autograph books, fully immersed in their own little magical world of holiday excitement and Christmas cheer. Laughter and excitement permeated throughout the room. They had autographs from Santa! There was something very unique and special about that.

"Like oh my gawd!" A curly blonde-haired girl's face lit up, her eyes sparkling as she held the autograph book over her heart, "I can't believe it!" She looked again at the scrolled message in red ink, just to make sure it was real.

"Like, I know right!" Another little girl agreed, feeling so proud that Santa had signed her book too.

"Whoa!" A little boy stared in disbelief, "I've got Santa's autograph!" he yelled, hands in the air, Rocky Balboa style.

"That's great! Did you get a chance to tell Santa what you wanted for Christmas while he signed your book?" his mom asked.

"Huh?" he said absently, still mesmerized by the signature in red. As far as he was concerned, he'd already gotten what he wished for. Santa had signed his very own autography book. Nothing was going to top that! Not for this eight-year-old.

ST. NICK SKEPTICS

I cannot tell you how many times that I've been complimented on everything from being the best and most authentic-looking Santa to having the most beautifully made Santa suit out there! Before I go any further, I must give all the thanks and kudos to my lovely wife who made sure that everything was in place: buttons, Velcro, safety pins, fake belly, perfect suspenders. Nothing got past her. She always went out of her way to be certain that I was the number one Santa Claus out there. A huge shout out to Mrs. Claus, who made sure everything ran smoothly and that I was always were I needed to be. As you can see, Mrs. Claus was much more than my right hand man (woman) - she actually doubled as a seamstress, events manager, coordinator, first assistant and in rare instances, personal body guard and high level security, if need be! You don't want to mess with Mrs. Claus.

I'm happy to report that I've been dubbed by some as being the most caring and patient Santa people had ever seen. Especially when it came to handling difficult situations in which children were experiencing the dreadful 'terrible twos'. Is it any wonder that children basically spend the first two years of their lives hearing their parents and other adults lecture them to stay away from people they don't know, don't take any candy from anyone, and don't talk to strangers? All of a sudden, Christmas arrives and in a contradictory twist, the children are handed off to a complete stranger, fully expecting them to accept and embrace that person with open arms. Particularly a big, fat stranger with a big, fat voice, in a big, fat chair wearing a big, fat red coat! The poor child is confused!

I recall one year when a mother came with her two-year-old, who stood off to the side, unsure of the strange man in the red suit.

"She won't go to you," the mother said flatly, glancing at her daughter who stood motionless, hands in her mouth, her eyes darting around not sure what to make of the festive wrapped presents and enticing, life-size snow covered gingerbread house.

"'She's shy."

"That's perfectly fine," I said. "Just go ahead and stand right over there for a few minutes. Do you want a picture of her with Santa?"

"I would like that," she said, not having much faith in the situation either way.

So I continued down the line visiting with the other kids, trying to make them feel at ease. I gave fist bumps and high-fives, shakas and handshakes, fully aware of the child watching me. Each child sat to take a Christmas picture with Santa for mom and dad, tutu and grandpa, uncle and aunty or anyone else who accompanied them. At one point, I decided to stretch my legs and took a short walk over to the roped-off section towards another child whose father cradled him as I said hello and tickled his cheek before walking back to my seat. After a few moments, we tried a second attempt with the little girl who had been silently watching. I held out my arms to the toddler and this time, to her mother's great amazement, she ran straight to me with open arms! Her mother was in shock.

"Yes!" she said victoriously after picking her jaw up off the ground.

AMAZING KIDS AND BRILLIANT SOULS

There is one encounter with a very special little boy that I'll never forget. He sat upon my lap and happily spoke of the toys and games that he wanted for Christmas.

"Have you been a good boy all year?"

"Yes, I have Santa," he promised with a nod.

"Have you been a big help to mom and dad in keeping your room clean and doing all your chores around the house?" I asked.

The little boy immediately stopped, turned to me very seriously and said, "Now Santa, you *know* that daddy died in the war," he reminded me.

To say my heart sank in that moment is an understatement. I was heartbroken and I needed to think fast. "You know," I began cautiously, "you're absolutely right. I *do* remember. But, with all the boys and girls I see throughout the world during Christmastime, I must have forgotten for a moment." I sighed, "but I do remember now."

The little boy nodded and gave a smile of approval.

I looked into his brave, little face and said, "Will you please forgive me for this mistake?" I asked.

"Of course, Santa," he said without a second thought. "You're forgiven. I know you're really busy." He smiled and left me with a huge bear hug.

What an amazing kid! And what a lesson learned for me. From that moment on, I realized I could never truly know what kind of life or circumstances the child had come from. From then on I would never again speak specifically (unless they brought it up first) of mom or dad, grandma or grandpa, or use any gender when addressing loved ones or significant others in their lives.

I had the pleasure of working with a wonderful children's hospital for about six years. What a joy it was to bring laughter and smiles to children that were in wheelchairs or had other challenging health conditions, some of whom couldn't speak at all.

"She's very happy, Santa." A mother smiled assuring me that her daughter was excited and happy to see Santa, her eyes reflecting excitement and joy.

"Well, that makes me very happy." I was filled with gratitude. It was an honor for me to be a part of and to make a small difference in the lives of these very special children. I will cherish and hold each and every one of them deep within my heart forever. They are true heroes and the epitome of courage by gracing us all and teaching us the gift of strength and love.

I had the honor of meeting many wonderful children at a special Christmas event held every year at a different function that I had been invited to for several years. I took my time at this particular event to greet or say hello to children who were there, wishing them all a very Merry Christmas. Many of the children had special needs, but all had great senses of humor and incredible attitudes. They happily interacted with me, although there were a few that could not. One little boy I remember well. He could not speak and relied on communicating through sign language. I sat in awe as I watched he and his mother interacting.

Santa is wishing you a very Merry Christmas. She signed, her fingers spelling out letters with rapid movements of expression.

Merry Christmas. Tell Santa I've been a good boy. He responded and signed with expertise.

Oh, Santa assures you he knows you've been. Her fingers, hands and facial expressions working in perfect collaboration. *What would you like for Christmas this year?*

I would like to read a fun book about airplanes.

"He says he'd like to have a fun book about airplanes." His mother relayed the message.

This just warmed my heart and I couldn't keep the tears from welling up in my eyes. "You tell him consider it done. Please let

* * *

him know how very proud Santa is of him too," I said, grateful for the opportunity to have spent a little time with this extraordinary boy. I was filled with so much inspiration as I watched the interaction between he and his mother that I later took it among myself to learn a tiny bit of sign language so that I could communicate directly to children with similar needs another time.

After this encounter, I learned to sign some basic words like Merry Christmas and what is your name, thank you and I love you. As time went on, it didn't stop there and I learned how to say a few words and phrases in Japanese, Samoan, Spanish, Hawaiian and even some Tahitian. I'd become somewhat of a multilingual Santa!

One of the parties I attended regularly over the years was with a family who at one time had just been blessed with a sweet newborn baby girl. I was their family Santa every year after she was born until the time she went off to college. Such a wonderful experience to watch children grow and change over the years. And through the years, it seemed the children were getting alarmingly smarter and paying closer attention to the fine details, much to Santa's dismay! We had just finished singing Christmas carols when I recited the last part of the famous Night before Christmas story.

"But I heard him exclaim, as he drove out of sight, Happy Christmas to all and to all a goodnight!"

"Let's give Santa a huge round of applause kids!" the children clapped and cheered. "We've got to say goodbye now because it's Santa's busiest night of the year!"

"Good-bye Santa!" Children's voices rang out through the room, "Thank you!" They jumped up and waved goodbye. When the coast was clear and I was safely outside, I re-entered the house through a side door as planned before making my way up the stairs to change clothes so I could re-join the party in progress. I quickly changed out of my Santa suit and into a pair of slacks with an extra Christmas party shirt I brought along. I carefully hung my Santa suit on special wooden hangers and folded the Santa hat before tucking it away with the rest of the suit. I then discreetly made my way back down the stairs to join the party that was in full swing.

"Merry Christmas, young man," I greeted, passing the little boy who was going up the stairs as I made my way down.

The boy passed me a step or two and stopped in his tracks. "Hey," he whispered, giving me a once over and taking a few steps back again. He stood right next to me now. "You know?" he squinted suspiciously, "you just missed Santa. He was just here," he informed me, fishing around for something. I held my breath fearing the worst, knowing that I was about to get reeled in.

"Oh, I know," I said in an attempt to cover my tracks. "I actually saw him before he took off and he said you kids were such a wonderful bunch of children to be with and he had such a fantastic time."

Like a seasoned detective from Hawaii Five-O, nothing was getting past this mini Steve McGarrett. "No," he shook his head, "you didn't see him," he concluded, "because *you* are him." He pointed to my shoes, "that's the exact pair of shoes Santa was wearing. I'm sure of it!"

Oh boy! Who in the world would ever think this young fella would be so incredibly observant to the point of calling out all the fine details in my shoes! That was it. Flash forward, I made an immediate appointment a few days later to have my boots customized with buttons to have the fur lined on them easily removed and easily replaced when needed.

I was also Santa at a private party for the friends and family of the manager for this same company over the course of the same seven or eight years. His home never ceased to amaze me, with its festive flare and warm aloha spirit. The children were always filled with excitement when I arrived and quick to join in with Christmas carols and familiar tunes they loved. There was always a wonderful sense of participation and collaboration when some of the children took hold of Santa's Christmas bells and added their own special take and riffs to the familiar jingle. We would gather around the tree and share eggnog and cookies, candy canes and cupcakes while we laughed, danced and sang the night away, right up until it was time to go. I told the kids that I was going to hop into my beautiful red sleigh as the reindeers stood at full attention. On Dasher, on Dancer, on Comet, on Cupid! On Prancer, on Donner, on Blitzen, and Vixen!

"What about Rudolph?" Children at various events over the years were flabbergasted when I didn't include him! "He's the main reindeer," they would say, disappointed. "You can't leave him out."

"Well, you see," I carefully explained, "Rudolph is not really needed in Hawaii, due to the beautiful weather we get all year around. Plus, we never have fog." I could see the wheels in their head turning as the reason made perfect sense to them.

"Oh," one little boy simply replied. "That's right."

"He needs to go to *snowy* places." His twin brother chimed in and emphasized, "like Russia."

"And China." The first twin gazed out into space.

"And...and...and..." the other continued swinging his legs back and forth, "Canada."

"Oh, and Alaska!" the twins brothers said in surprised unison, then stopped to stare at each other before bowling over in a burst of uncontrollable laughter that brought both brothers to their knees - one was actually rolling on the floor at my feet.

Another time I remember well was when a little boy about five years old came up to me. I asked him what his name was and if he liked school. After a few minutes of chatting, I asked what he wanted for Christmas.

The boy hung his head and hesitated, then reached into his pocket and pulled out some money. "Santa," he began, "I haven't been a very good boy this year." Obviously he felt bad, "do you think this can tide me over till after Christmas?"

I looked into his eyes and gently replied, "No. I'm sorry. Santa cannot take any money. Thank you very much. But can you be good for the rest of the year?"

"Yes, I can!" he promised.

"Will you help around the house, pick up your toys, eat your vegetables, and brush your teeth twice a day?"

"Yes Santa, I can do that!" he said, a spark of hope in his voice.

"Then I want you to take that money and buy something for someone special for Christmas, or even spend it on something fun for yourself. Maybe some bubble gum or candy or something you really like and we'll call it even. How does that sound?"

"That sounds good, Santa." He smiled, "Thank you, Santa!" he waved, hopped off my lap and sprinted to his parents with a renewed sense of hope in every step.

The upside to the story? Another child leaves, happy, content and filled with Christmas joy. The downside? I was out five bucks! But ho hum, all's well that ends well.

I had been the Santa at a company Christmas party for a total of eight years. The site was located in a ritzy, expensive part of town, with beautiful homes and luxurious estates surrounding the area. One year, I had a young man approach me who was a little older than the rest of the kids. He didn't want to sit down, but instead stood next to me very proper with a nice vest and suit on. I figured he was definitely from around that area.

"So have you decided what you want for Christmas?" I casually opened the conversation.

"I really want a drone."

"A drone?" I leaned back with raised eye brows at his mother who was motioning for me to say no!

"Let me tell you something," I said. "In order to fly a drone, you need to have permission from the Federal Aviation Administration (FAA). You're restricted to areas that are not anywhere near backyards or swimming pools and you must abide by strict no fly zone regulations." I laid out the rules noticing his newfound decision to perhaps do more research and decide finally to wait a while longer.

"You know, I never thought of that." He said of his newfound enlightenment on drones. "I think I will wait for a while. Thank you Santa." He said, satisfied with his decision while his mother gave a grateful thumbs up from the background.

I've said before, time and time again, what I love about Christmas: the lights, the garland, the decorations, the wreaths, the way people change their attitudes. I fully believe Christmas is much more than a day, a week, a month, it's more of an attitude and a state of mind. During the holidays, I love when people want to do good for others in this state of mind without even thinking about it - how I wish this could last all year long.

I remember a little four-year-old boy speaking up as he stood in line. He mentioned how long his Christmas list was, as his voice echoed through the air. "Come on up here," I smiled when he approached.

"Santa, I brought my list." He held up the very large list that was actually taller than him! "It's lots of pages." He stated the obvious before going down the entire list.

"May I please have this list?" I asked. "Let me take it back with me to the North Pole and have my elves check it to make sure we can get everything on the list for you?"

"Yes, Santa!" he was ecstatic and gave a big hug and kiss before running off to his mother waiting nearby. "Have a good Christmas, Santa!" he said. He then paused a moment, "Santa? Please *don't forget* me, okay!"

I laughed a real, jolly laugh and promised him, I could *never* forget him!

PALAKA SANTA SUIT

A local favorite here in the Hawaiian Islands is the palaka Santa suit – checkered red and white - that was especially made just for me. I had four different suits made, all in my size! I want to give a huge shout-out to the wonderful woman and seamstress who was responsible for making me look so absolutely incredible! Her talent was much appreciated by both me and my wife. Palaka is a gingham material that comes in almost every color imaginable. The cowboys of old Hawaii always wore palaka patterned shirts. I was fortunate to have had slippers custom made just for me with the palaka material that strapped over the toes. The fur used with the palaka Santa suit was also brought in special from the mainland. This truly was a gorgeous suit and definitely a local favorite.

MISSED OPPORTUNITIES

A life-long friend of my wife and I called to make arrangements for an upcoming *after* Christmas party and wanted Santa to show up, too. Keep in mind, 99.9% of all the events and Christmas parties that I've attended have been held in the evening or at night. Our family friend told us to show up at a particular hotel pool side at "7:30" the day *after* Christmas. No problem...until the phone rang early that same morning at 7:30 am.

"Where in the world are you, Santa?" the voiced blared through the phone speaker, jolting me awake.

"What?" I replied somewhat surprised, "Where am I? Why, I'm at home."

"Why are you at home?"

"What do you mean?"

"We had an appointment for this morning at 7:30!" she said, affirming the calendar in front her with the 26th of December circled in red. "I have it right here. Don't tell me you forgot?"

"No. I didn't forget." I quickly replied, fearing for my life (Kidding!) "I thought you meant 7:30 in the evening?"

"No!" she said. "I told you A.M. Hello! That means m-o-r-n-i-n-g!"

For the life of me, I couldn't remember her saying it was in the morning instead of the evening. Looking back on it now, this would have been a great photo shoot and truly is one of those missed opportunities that we should have followed up on. We should have rescheduled and planned to do it again and perhaps use the photos the following year or in the future. Oh well, so much for this ("Kapakahi" lopsided, crocked in Hawaiian) communication!

What's so big about this photo shoot? Well, it was a unique in that with all the hustle and bustle of the holiday season and gifts, wrapping, visitors, parties and events in which Santa and his elves are tasked with every year, our family friend - in her many moments of brilliant creativity - had the fantastic idea to have a picture of Santa taken the day *after* Christmas. This photo would have showcased a worn out and very exhausted Santa sleeping soundly in a lounge chair with pillows propped up around, having just traveled the world delivering gifts to children everywhere. Each party guest would have the option of taking a photo with Santa, but of course instead of sitting on my lap, they'd just sit next to me, while I snored away. Unfortunately it didn't happen, but I know if it did, it would have been a really cute photo and loved by everyone, no doubt!

One of my biggest wishes and something I've always dreamt of doing was to be the Santa who rode in on the sleigh during the grand finale at the end of the famous Macy's Thanksgiving Day Parade held every year in New York City. How amazing that would have been and regretfully will never come to fruition – but if only it had. Between my wife's limitless dedication and my complete commitment to the role of Santa, you can bet your bottom dollar, *this* Santa would not only have been the best Hawaiian Santa, but would have put Hawaii on the map, no doubt.

CHRISTMAS TOWN

Interestingly, I went to Alaska one year to a town that was called - you guessed it - Christmas Town! Everything in this town has to do with Christmas, from the streets, to the buildings, to every name for every store! In one general store they had a big Santa chair with a big sign that said

Please do not sit in chair,

I'm taking care of the reindeers and

won't be back until tomorrow!

After showing the store owners some of my photos that were taken of me as Santa at different parties, they got really excited and insisted on having me pose for a few photos while sitting in their Santa chair. Luckily for me, I was used to traveling with my Hawaiian palaka Santa suit and conveniently put it on before taking the seat that, up until now, no one had permission to sit in. Everyone we were traveling with insisted on having a photo with Santa, including the store owners. People started trailing in wanting to see what all the commotion was about and wasted no time getting a photo taken with Santa, too. The children got a kick out of it and quickly sat on my lap for a picture with mom and dad. All the employees wanted in on the action and rushed over to have a picture too, making sure not to be left out of all the fun! All in all it ended up being such a fun experience where – although thousands of miles away – Santa felt right at home.

YEAR 'ROUND RESTAURANT FUN

Many years ago I worked for a company that had a chain of popular family style restaurants where I was employed as manager for about five years. We took great pride in decorating the interior of the dining area as well as the outside displays. Every holiday we would spring into action, bringing in multiple prompts for the upcoming celebration. It didn't matter what holiday it was, we would honor them all. There were pink and red roses on each table with swaying helium-filled heart shaped balloons in February. Green top-hat wearing elves littered with clovers and shamrocks in March. In April, it turned into a family affair with my youngest children helping out during the Easter celebrations, showing up in full costume from head to toe! Imagine the customers surprise when a floppy-eared, fluffy-tailed, pink life-size Easter bunny hopped in to deliver a special Easter egg – usually filled with chocolate or jelly beans - just for them! Years later, my daughter complained sorely that she had lost about five pounds after stepping out of the Easter suit one day, as the costume was made of thick, heavy material that made it somewhat difficult to walk in, let alone hop.

Although Christmas was always my favorite holiday, a close second was Halloween. With the same amount of passion, creativity, and enthusiasm I poured into my Santa role, the same was true for my Halloween costumes. Initially, many of the restaurant employees didn't want to dress up or be involved with any of the holiday costumes or celebrations. Although employees reluctantly agreed to participate and dress up at first, their tips were doubled, to their happy surprise, in addition to having a fantastic time! I've shown up for work as everything from a Navajo Indian, beautifully adorned with a real, authentic eagle feathered head dress that went pass my knees and ran almost the entire length of my legs. A few years later, I dressed as one of the lead singers from a popular 1970s rock group. We hired a make-up artist to paint my face with the iconic all-white with black diamond patterns over my eyes, before sporting the all black pants and shirt, complete with a black and red satin-lined cape. It was quite a costume and loved by everyone, especially rock fans! Another year, I opted for a more traditional, scary Halloween character to dress up as. I chose a frightening werewolf costume with a face mask worthy of being cast in your next box office movie smash hit. It was amazing and gave lots of unsuspecting folks the scare of a lifetime; sneaking up behind some and scaring the beejezus out of them while others I simply tapped on the shoulders for a quick scream before they bolted off and ran for their lives - all in fun of course!

For Thanksgiving, we thoroughly enjoyed creating a horn-of-plenty made of chicken wire stuffed with tissue paper in fall colors of brown, yellow, orange, and red before placing corn, pumpkins and other vegetables and edible goodies inside to spill out over the counter, giving it a feel of grateful abundance. That was the beginning of a fun tradition, and I was pleasantly surprised at the level of participation and anticipation when all of the different holidays rolled around the following year, with many employees bringing their own creative ideas to the table, even willing to work overtime, and took so much joy in deciding then creating what they were planning to wear far before the actual day arrived!

By the time December rolled around, the restaurant had been transformed into a winter wonderland. The windows were sprayed with white foam-like snow while snowflakes dangled from the table and counter tops. Stockings with each employee's name on it, hung by garland throughout the restaurant. Doors where wrapped like over grown Christmas presents with stringing lights of red and green twinkling bright on the pretty tall Christmas tree near the entrance. I – being Santa of course – would make an appearance during this festive time – on my days off from the restaurant- to stop by, in full costume to wish all the employees a Merry Christmas and of course the lucky few diners who were not only surprised to see Santa but super happy to chit chat with him and shake his hand. Such fun!

HOSPITAL VISITS

Some years later – still under the same restaurant chain – I took another manager position at a different location in Aina Haina. At some point during this time, I fell ill and was diagnosed with infectious pneumonia and ended up in the intensive care unit (ICU). I was hospitalized for three weeks during the Christmas holidays as my prognosis worsened. It was Christmas Eve when my doctor made an urgent phone call to my wife and urged her to bring our children into the hospital to see me as, I had taken a turn for the worse. The doctors feared I wouldn't live to see Christmas Day. Well live I did, through the grace of God! I will forever be grateful and have enormous gratitude to all the doctors and nurses who gave the best round the clock care to me. When the ordeal was over and I finally had a clean bill of health, I wanted so much to do something for the good folks there who had in fact saved my life. But, what could I do? A simple thank you would not be good enough for me. I had to do more.

The following year, I decided to stop into this hospital as Santa to wish the doctors and nurses there a Merry Christmas and to thank them for all they had done for me. I took a few hours to go to different floors, wishing everyone there a wonderful holiday. I couldn't thank the staff enough for all they had done for me and my family. I'm happy to report that this wonderful visit would become a tradition and for the next four decades - yep, for 43 years I have devoted my time as Santa during the holidays to stop in and thank the amazing doctors and nurses at this particular hospital. Without them, I simply wouldn't be here. I will forever be one grateful Santa!

I was fortunate to visit a prominent military hospital in Hawaii, wishing everyone there a very Merry Christmas. What a wonderful experience and an honor it was to be able to tell folks in beds, wheelchairs, and traction that Santa had come to wish them a very Merry Christmas and that they were not forgotten. To stand next to a soldier and just hold their hand and listen to how thankful they were and how grateful they were that Santa had come by to see them for Christmas brought tears to my eyes and certainly was one of the highlights of my Santa experiences. Many of the men and women didn't have any family in Hawaii, and Santa was the only visit they got for Christmas, besides the doctors and nurses. They never let me forget how thankful they were for such a brief, yet meaningful visit that many times lifted their spirits and warmed my heart. All the gratitude, love and appreciation that these wounded soldiers expressed in being visited by Santa, even in the mist of their unfortunate predicaments, was extraordinary. Sometimes they joked around, but many times they spoke with such depth and emotion in tearful appreciation. Numerous times, walking out of the hospital after visiting with them, felt like I was walking on clouds, the impact of the visit and sharing this experience was almost surreal. I always looked forward to seeing and speaking with soldiers and their families year after year. Just before my the fifth year of visiting, I called the hospital like I had done the previous years to arrange a time for Santa's Christmas visit. Only this time, I did not receive the usual anticipated greeting from years prior.

"Unfortunately," the woman said in an apologetic tone, "we're not going to be having you here this year."

To say I was shocked is an understatement, as I couldn't for the life of me figure out why in the world they wouldn't want Santa to come for a visit? "What?" I couldn't believe what she was saying. "Why?"

"Well," she sounded defeated, "we have a new commandant who doesn't particularly care for Christmas and thinks all it is, is one big distraction."

"Well," I pondered a moment, "I won't tell you what I *really* think, because simply put, I represent Santa. But, I can say this, you are wrong. Everyone there has been so very grateful and thankful that I took time to come up there to wish them a Merry Christmas. You tell that new commandant that I dare him to walk around and wish everyone a Merry Christmas and to truthfully explain why Santa won't be there this year," I challenged. "Why Santa won't be there because of his own stubbornness!" I hung up the phone. I never heard from that hospital again, which was very sad because it was such an important part of my life.

OLD ELF

I owned a 24-year-old white Toyota truck. For the last seven years, my license plate said OLD ELF. Six years ago, I painted the truck bright red and the pipe rack stand pure white. In November and December, I put a 28 inch decorated wreath on the front grill. It was fun driving to parties or around town and seeing folks giving shaka signs and asking me to pull over so they could get a picture with me. When I had to stop at any red light, believe it or not, people would take the opportunity to jump out of their cars and trucks, come over to my truck, give a holiday shaka, take a quick picture of me, then hop back into their vehicles, *all* before the light turned green!

IT'S A BIRD! IT'S A PLANE! IT'S SANTA!

While being the Santa for a large shopping center on the windward side, we flew in on a helicopter for three years in a row! We landed in an empty field where a building and a well-known store now stands. During our second year, as expected, we arrived on the helicopter to an excited crowd of approximately 200 people waving from the ground below. We could see the fire department there for safety reasons, in addition to the local news station who were excited to capture the live festive events unfolding to feature in their holiday segment of the evening news. We landed amongst the cheering crowd, then carefully made our way out of the helicopter. Immediately, we were ushered quickly away from the rotating blades of the propeller and over to a safer, all clear designated area. Happily, everything had gone according to plan, when suddenly, to my great horror the wig I had worn, including the beard (I was still wearing a fake one at that particular time) had flown completely off my head! Unfortunately, when the helicopter lifted up to leave, the heavy wind force of the propeller when circling around my head had taken part of Santa's costume with it! Well, you'd never seen so many people rush into action! As if an act of faith, miraculously within seconds, a crowd of 'assistants and elves' gathered around me as I knelt down on my knees and completely covered me from view while magically reattaching the wig, beard and hat back on asap within seconds! We continued on with our meet and greet with Santa and everyone enjoyed the festive event as if nothing had happened. I began to wonder if anyone saw anything at all? If they did, you couldn't tell. They were oblivious, to my happy surprise. All I saw and heard all morning were screaming, excited and happy children and am happy to report, although there was an abrupt unexpected start to *that* day, it sure ended with a blast of fun.

SCARY SANTA

There are many places and companies that I had worked for or had done work for throughout the years. A frame company – owned by a very dear friend – my doctor's office, my wife's favorite hair salon, the local dry cleaner, who had been so generous and many times took my Santa suit in for a thorough clean, with no charge to us! There were so many people and places to visit and I felt an enormous sense of gratitude to be able to share a laugh, a smile and to greet as many people as I could and to say thank you and a very Merry Christmas to them all.

One year, on my way home from a company party, I was driving near to Kaneohe and had a great idea to quickly drop by and do a surprise visit for some friends. For starters, I had the classic Santa Christmas jingle bells attached to my suit, which by the way, you can hear from six blocks away! I walked up to the door and knocked. No one. I reached down and found the handle unlocked, so I let myself in. I got about three fourths of the way in when suddenly their son came out of the room and OMG! He almost had a heart attack!

"Santa!" he almost screamed. "You scared me to death!"

"Well, I'm so sorry, it's not like I snuck in, you could hear the bells and the knocking from a mile away," I laughed. Later he called his mom who wasn't there at the time and told her his predicament.

"I told you to lock that door when you're home alone!" she scolded.

"Mom!" he reasoned, "it's *Santa*!"

"Oh," she paused. "Okay, well in that case, it's fine." She laughed.

YOU DON'T BELIEVE IN SANTA?

Every so often I hear the dreadful *I don't believe in Santa* line. Sadly, there are folks who simply do not believe. They think that Santa is not real. But, I can attest right here and now - my eight children, 18 grandchildren, and six great-grandchildren would disagree!

When folks tell me they don't believe, I then ask the person why and they explain that they didn't get the car they had asked for last year or something like that. Well, believe me you, I always have the perfect answer for both men and women.

"Well, I looked at the list, in fact I even checked it twice and although you weren't at the top, you were on the naughty list. So, I don't think you're going to get the car this year either."

"What!" One gentleman hollered before giving a loud laugh, "Don't tell me that!" He shook his head in disbelief.

"You be good." I pointed at him, "then check back with me next year." I laughed a jolly laugh before everyone chimed in and did the same.

• • •

CHRISTMAS CHEER - IT DOESN'T TAKE MUCH

I have been in homes that have so many decorations that there is hardly any place at all to sit. Even in small spaces, families are always happy to have Santa there, even though it was sometimes uncomfortable as everyone watched every move I made - how I sat, where I placed my feet and hands, or even how I situated my hat on my head. But, as long as the children were happy, I was happy.

I've been in homes where there was only a tiny table, or maybe a small pre-decorated tree to plug in, but the families truly love and want to have Santa there. At one home, the family had wrapped three tiny gifts by the tree for the kids in the spirit of Christmas. It was amazing to see that the children were not disappointed by the number of gifts, but rather expressed their love for Santa by sharing hugs of gratitude. This little family of four, a single mother with three kids, clearly didn't have much, but they were such happy and joyful children none the less. They embodied the true meaning of Christmas with hearts filled with

Christmas spirit, cheer and gratitude. This is what made playing the role of Santa so special for me and visiting them will remain one of the best experiences I've ever encountered.

CHRISTMAS DECORATIONS

Santa's house in Kailua, Hawaii is a wonderful Christmas wonderland, full of the Christmas spirit. Christmas lights adorning our coconut tree, which is 50 feet tall, was one of the fun highlights of our decorations, which also included festive Christmas lights around the gazebo and carport and Christmas garland that bordered the entire house, topped off with a festive five foot tall Christmas wreath out front on the fence. A timer was set to turn on all the lights, giving the house and yard such a warm, beautiful Christmas glow.

Our upstairs living room boasted even more decorations, to include a standing six foot tall Santa holding a Christmas tree with lights and a six foot tall nutcracker soldier with a top hat and lights. One of our very favorite of all the decorations was the constantly growing Christmas village, expanding in size with each passing year. In our family room downstairs, we displayed not one, but four layers of a beautifully decorated and detailed ceramic Christmas village. The top level or shelf was decorated to look like the North Pole with about eight houses, a barn for the reindeer, a lighthouse, Santa's workshop, toyshop, candy cane shop, Mr. and Mrs. Claus winter cottage and Santa's treehouse, including eight reindeer pulling a sleigh full of toys. Of course there were trees, snow on the ground, mailboxes, street lamps and more.

The second shelf of the little village was a boathouse and a lighthouse – on both sides of this particular shelf were two separate lighthouses – one lighthouse to represent the east coast and the other lighthouse representing the west coast. There was also a police station, fire house, barber shop, post office, a church, a bakery shop and many more homes and cottages.

On the next shelf, there was another lighthouse, more family homes, two churches, toyshops, bike shop, museums, a bookstore, a bank, and a library. One year, we also had a train that ran on tracks around the entire town, with two of the flat cars filled with wrapped presents! Being from the islands, we always made sure that every shelf of the little Santa village donned a special Christmas decoration unique to Hawaii.

Every place in our home was decorated with a wide variety of wonderful Santas collected from all the exciting places we have traveled to throughout the world. There was no way we could put up just one single Christmas tree during the holidays, as there were so many ornaments and decorations to display. During any given year, our household would have at least three different Christmas trees. We always had a traditional tree with lights and fun decorations. One of the favorite trees displayed the many different ornaments we collected from every place we had traveled to. There were ornaments and different kinds of Santa's from Russia, Canada, Europe, China, Japan, Alaska, Seattle, North Carolina, San Francisco, Catalina, Las Vegas, Panama, Spain, Italy, London, France and much more.

FAMILY, FRIENDS, FUN!

Several times as the years went by we rented a school bus for the family. One particular time, we had about 35 people with us. Friends, family, brothers, sisters, kids, grandchildren and even great-grandchildren. I wore my palaka vest over a white shirt, along with my hat and of course my jingle bells. As we set off to go see the beautiful Christmas lights in Honolulu, we were dubbed 'Uncle Santa' with my lovely wife being 'Aunty Elf '.

Anytime we went anywhere only partially dressed in costume, it was always:

"Hi Uncle Santa! Hi Aunty Elf!" Our family friends and acquaintances would happily greet us when boarding the bus. When we finally reached our destination and got off the bus, folks would carry on the newfound tradition and continue to address us as Uncle Santa and Aunty Elf! It was cute and always made us smile, a feeling of ohana being shared among so many and at times with complete strangers.

Speaking of family, once I was at home getting dressed to go to a function at a popular outdoor shopping center. At that time, I

CHRISTMAS STORIES WITH SANTA

was the new proud grandfather of the first two grandchildren. They were used to seeing me in full costume in the Santa suit with the bells before I headed out the door.

"Hi Papa," they said grinning. "We know it's you," they announced.

"Yes. It's me," I said. "But when I'm in my costume wearing my Santa suit *please* call me Santa. Okay?"

"Okay," they shrugged.

We got to the Christmas party at the shopping center and I went up on stage to sit in my nice big chair. The children lined up as usual and came up on stage to chat for a little while before helping themselves to one of the candy canes and cookies from the Santa bag.

"Can I take two candy canes, Santa?" one girl asked. "My little sister isn't feeling well today. She has a bad cold, but I want to give her a candy cane when we go home."

"Of course you can," I agreed instantly. "You tell sister that I hope she feels much better and to have a very Merry Christmas."

"Thank you Santa. I will." She hurried off with the double treats as I waved goodbye. I turned to see two siblings waltzing up onto the stage and recognized the happy duet immediately.

"Papa!" they both ran over to me. "Papa!" they screamed and plopped right onto my lap.

I laughed a jolly laugh and made sure they got their treats. As they were exiting the stage, I whispered to them, "remember now kids, it's Santa."

Oops! They quickly covered their mouths as they made their way off the stage giggling, "Bye, Papa Santa!"

With the holidays being jammed packed with so many private parties, holiday events and corporate Christmas holiday functions, I always looked forward to the party that was put together by one of my dear church member friends. He would host a wonderful party in a beautiful home filled with all of his wonderful children and grandchildren. I looked forward to seeing them every year, as it was always a warm and welcoming and very festive atmosphere, the Christmas cheer resonating throughout the night.

One year, I could hear the children singing Christmas carols all the way from the street. I held on to my Santa belt with the attached jingle bells, so as not to make a sound. The singing got louder as my friend and his wife encouraged the children to sing so that Santa could possibly hear them and show up! Well, hear them he did!

"Ho! Ho! Ho!" I gave a jolly laugh. "Merry Christmas! Mele Kalikimaka!" I waved to the astonished children who were by now screaming with excitement when I walked through the door. What a wonderful night it was. We sang and danced for some time before each child came up to sit with Santa one by one. We laughed and they promised to be good for the entire new year that was fast approaching. Before each child left, we made sure to get a Christmas photo with Santa to take home to their families.

I remember clearly, this one particular year I took the time to recite The Night Before Christmas story to the children. "Now, I know you've all heard the story before, but I want to tell you one more time…" the children sat wide eyed. Quiet. Watching. Listening.

"Twas the night before Christmas and all through the house, not a creature was stirring not even a mouse. The stockings were hung by the chimney with care, in hopes that St. Nicholas soon would be there."

As I continued with the story you could hear a pin drop, it was so quiet. By the time the story had ended, some of the children had snuggled up comfortably with their moms and dads, while others sat glued, frozen in time, watching me and mesmerized at every move I made.

"Now, kids," I whispered, all eyes on me. "It's Christmas Eve, and you know what that means." I nodded to the excited faces. "You need to go to bed soon because when you awake in the morning, I will have left some fun presents and gifts for each and every one of you. And that goes for you too mom, dad, grandma and grandpa." The children clapped and cheered between sleepy yawns. "So let's get everything here cleaned up, put everything away, and please be sure to leave at least one carrot each for the reindeers," I reminded them, "and for me, one chocolate chip cookie and just one small glass of milk. Because by the time I get to the other houses, I'm way too stuffed with all the cookies and milk I've had there, too!"

There's a home I always went to visit over the years. About the second year I was there, the little boy – who's now all grown up – came to the door when I showed up for Christmas that year.

"Who's there?" he asked after hearing the knock.

"Ho, ho, ho!" I greeted, before the door swung open and I was met with excitement and anticipation.

"Mom! Dad!" he yelled to his parents, "Ho, Ho is here!" he screamed excitedly.

With each passing year, whenever I showed up at the house for Christmas, they would hear me greeting from outside with bells and a jolly Ho, Ho, Ho! They'd come rushing out to greet me with an excited announcement to everyone who was within a one mile radius that *Ho, Ho was here! Ho, Ho was here!* It would become the family's very own unique staple name for me. Quite funny and always a laugh. Even to this day, we still get together with the family. In fact, we recently went to a brunch luncheon and the boy – who's all grown up now – greeted me saying, "Ho, Ho! Ho, Ho! I'm glad you're here! So good to see you!"

TURNING POINT 2015

At some point during the year of 2015, I was busy in my workshop working on a koa table top, doing some final cuts before putting it together. As I worked diligently on this particular piece, I suddenly stepped back, startled at what I was seeing. Out of nowhere, what was once regular, normal vision had frighteningly become not one, but two of everything! I was seeing double! I shut everything down and cleaned everything up that had been covered with sawdust. When I was done, I went in and called my wife who was at work and told her my predicament.

"Make an appointment immediately with the eye doctor," she insisted.

When I saw my doctor we ended up opting for surgery as my right eye muscle had become weak. Over time I was forced to deal with other ongoing health issues. I was experiencing increasing pain in my neck and lower back, which had been painful on and off for many years. When I finally had x rays done, the doctor was astonished by the results. He told me I had three vertebrae in my neck and five in my lower back that had no cartilage – bone on bone - and what's worse, the bones had fused themselves together! He continued to inform me that the arthritis I already had was causing the growth of bone spurs, which unfortunately are poking against the skin leading to so much trouble.

Consequently, my wife and I made the difficult decision to close down Damaged Branches Custom Framing as well as agreeing to hang up Santa's hat for good. I sent out a letter to all of my lovely, wonderful friends, family and customers who I had done business with throughout the years informing them that I would be retiring as Santa. I cannot tell you the outpouring of support and overwhelming response that I received as a result of that letter. It seemed that everyone I'd done business with over the many years of playing Santa had reached out. The coordinator out at one of the hotels told me when she received the letter she called a quick meeting and took a moment to read it to the employees. When she was done reading the letter, she said there wasn't a dry eye in the house.

A HUI HOU

Being Santa has been a tremendously huge part of my life. Everywhere I go, even now, someone, somewhere will stop me. "You're that Santa!" they say, recognizing me from days gone by as I still have my beard – although it's shorter now. We usually chit chat for a moment and they reminisce about the fun party they saw me at or the event they attended, with wonderful, nostalgic memories of laughter and fun.

Over the years, I've played Santa for parties with as few as 10 people, to larger events with guest lists ranging well over 500. The one thing that has remained consistent and constant through the years is the feeling of joy I experience in seeing the spark in children's eyes. It truly is one of the greatest Christmas gifts ever.

In a very real sense, at times, playing the role of Santa has been equivalent to being a celebrity. But, in my opinion, so much more rewarding. I've done my very best and have always given 110% to playing this remarkable, jolly character. As I reflect back over the years I must say I have been truly blessed. I have thoroughly enjoyed this gift of playing such a significant role and absolutely loved being a representative of the jolly, old elf himself, the wonderful old St. Nick.

And with that being said, we draw to a close a most unforgettable chapter in my life. With much admiration, much love and with much appreciation of being a part of the best known person throughout the world, Jolly Old St. Nick. I say to you all Aloha!

Mele Kalikimaka is the thing to say
On a bright Hawaiian Christmas Day
That's the island greeting that we send to you
From the land where palm trees sway

Here we know that Christmas will be green and bright
The sun will shine by day and all the stars at night
Mele Kalikimaka is Hawaii's way
To say Merry Christmas to you

Mele Kalikimaka is the thing to say
On a bright Hawaiian Christmas Day
That's the island greeting that we send to you
From the land where palm trees sway

Here we know that Christmas will be green and bright

The sun will shine by day and all the stars at night

Mele Kalikimaka is Hawaii's way

To say Merry Christmas to you

Here we know that Christmas will be green and bright

The sun will shine by day and all the stars at night

Mele Kalikimaka is Hawaii's way

To say Merry Christmas, a very very Merry Merry Christmas

To say Merry Christmas to you!

A huge Mahalo and a very Mele Kalikimaka from the Hawaiian Palaka Santa.

Jolly Old St. Nick

Santa with the Christmas Canoe Crew head to shore of screaming fans on Waikiki Beach.

Jolly Old St. Nick

Palaka Santa. Waikiki Beach.

Lillie Santa Inc.

Santa Money

Cheering crowd welcomes Santa. Waikiki Beach.

My beautiful pet eagle, Goldie.

Mr. and Mrs. Claus

With a heavy heart after 45 + years playing the part of the most jolly person in the world, Old St. Nick, I'll be hanging up my red Palaka Santa suit so I can spend time with my family during the Christmas Holidays.

It was truly a wonderful experience to see the excitement in the eyes of little children as they whispered softly to me of what they wished for at Christmas. This interaction gave me the opportunity to learn a few things from a child's point of view that I would not have thought of otherwise.

Thank you for allowing me to be part of your organization and/or family that I am forever grateful for and will always remember your support.

Me Ke Aloha Pumehana,
(With Warm Regards)

Old. St. Nick
Donald Boyce

Made in the USA
San Bernardino, CA
23 November 2019